Feasting
on the
Poisoned
Pie

THOMAS VICK
the SIN-seared Questioner

INKS
BINDINGS

Inks and Bindings
888-290-5218
www.inksandbindings.com
orders@inksandbindings.com

Contents

The Thunderous Introduction

I was sleeping when I heard the loudest thunder I have ever witnessed. It shook the entire house and I was instantly awake. I didn't know what happened. There was no indication of an advancing thunder storm. Could this be a bomb that just exploded in the neighborhood? Without conscious effort of my own, it felt like I was lifted up and moved outside, right through the walls! Horrified, I looked back toward my bed and saw a body lying there. It was my body that I had washed, and clothed, and fed for so many years! What is going on?

I looked at where my hands have always been and did see a form that resembled what I had seen just before this sudden event began. My new form was similar but yet different with a dimension which is hard to describe. The thought occurred to me that this could be my soul. I reached up to my face and I could feel my touch. Just a few moments ago I was in that body that was still there on that bed. That body had a leg missing due to a serious accident a few years ago. The pain of that loss of limb had always been constant, sometimes very agonizing. That remembrance made me move my hands down to my leg. I was shocked when I could feel both legs without the pain! Even though I had a complete body now, or should I say form, I was horrified at what I was experiencing.

Then I heard the sound of voices that was rapidly getting closer. There was crying, screaming, more like wailing! The sound was so gruesome that I shuddered in my new form, which I thought must be what I heard preachers call a soul. I realized that this soul could see, could feel, could think, and could remember the past. And now with the horrifying screams, I concluded it could also hear. Every sense that was capable just a few moments ago was now amplified to a greater dimension than I had ever known before. Then my eyes saw a sea, or should I say, an ocean of people.

As far as I could see, there were forms just like me. They too, didn't have flesh and blood like I used to have. It became clear to me then that these too were souls and this event must be what I had heard of years ago, a Judgment to come. At the time I thought it was an imagination of religious fanatics. Seeing and hearing that wailing around me, I quickly took inventory of what I had done in my life. I tried living a good life. I believed in God, that there actually was a God. I heard someone say that I needed to say out loud, verbally, that "Jesus Christ is Lord", and I would be saved from the place called, Hell! I did do all of that. But the screaming all around me became so loud that I couldn't even continue with my thoughts.

A voice much louder than the clap of thunder just moments ago, shouted, "SILENCE!" It was so loud that it shook everything that was created by this powerful voice. I realized that I had just heard God for the first time, and I got scared. Unsure of where my soul stood before his laws, I tried to whimper, but I could not make a sound! Fear that I had never experienced before gripped me, but I still couldn't scream! I noticed the deathly silence of all these souls. There were millions, actually billions, of souls which I could never count. And yet with this unfathomable amount of souls, it was absolutely quiet.

I cowered down drastically when that same voice boomed out the command, "Let the final Judgment begin!" I wanted to hide. One name was called out each time this voice spoke, which shuddered within every soul. The soul disappeared to his fate and another name was called. Compared to my former experience of what I thought life was, this event was taking days. However, compared to eternity, it was not even one second of time.

The name of a pastor who I had heard on TV was called. I thought surely that he would go to heaven. Instead, I heard that man claim he had done many wonderful things. He was pleading with God about his accomplishments. Then horrified, we all heard the voice thunder the words, "DEPART FROM ME YOU THAT WORKED AND LIVED IN SIN!" I dreaded the thought, that if this famous pastor just went to hell, how could I ever stand before God, justified?

Chapter One

Basics of Life & Principles

People are dying around us constantly which is normal. What is ironic though is that whenever someone dies, the comment heard <u>almost</u> always is, "They are in a better place." The reason I didn't say just "always", (instead of <u>almost</u> always), is because I'm still trying to find a situation where the survivors say, "They are now in a worse place!" You meet evil people and assume that the deceased must have been similar because of relationship. And yet these evil people who are doing evil acts still claim that their loved one went to heaven. How can this be true that everyone goes to heaven? Is there anyone that goes to hell?

Many individuals avoid anything to do with religion because of some religious "Bible-Thumper" that beats the stranger up with how they are supposed to live. The stranger evaluates that religious individual and then compares himself to him. Have you ever witnessed some religious person that might hold a prominent position in a church, go totally Godless in behavior and speech when something went wrong? He accidentally smashed his thumb with a hammer. Instantly the angry vocabulary of profanity comes forth that would make a drunken sailor blush. The sinner looks on in amazement and decides that if this man goes to heaven, he himself would have a much better chance of heaven even if he never went to church.

This book is not intended to be a "Bible-thumping" book. Instead, the desire for it is to make it live up to the name of "Questioner". Throughout this short book, there will be a lot of questions encouraging the reader to decide what they want to gravitate towards. As long as the reader ponders each topic, and then makes a deliberate and solid decision, then this book will be a success. It is far more important to make a definite personal decision, than trying to live under the beliefs of others. If some reader has already made a decision of throwing this book away after only reading The Introduction, or even these first three paragraphs, then the book has already succeeded.

The purpose for writing this book is to present various ideas or words that were written about 2000 years ago. How those words all fit together in daily life, and how to evaluate or interpret them is the part that you have to decide. I don't want you to accept what I believe, unless you have thought extensively about each topic and confirmed it for yourself. Making you seriously ponder the "road map" of how to get to heaven is this book's goal. If you are bored with this topic already and don't want to continue, then I want to thank you for already making a decision which makes this book a success. If however, you are eager to think and then

decide on the most important decision in your life, I
beg you to continue reading

Chapter Two

Is There a God?

There are laws of Probabilities. What that means is that you put one single dice (die) in a plastic cup, shake it, and then roll the die onto the table. The law of Probabilities is that you have one chance in six that you end up with a six. If you rolled the die eighteen times, you should average about three times with a six. But what if you used two dice? Correct me if I'm wrong in the Laws of Probabilities. I believe using two dice, you must multiply six chances times six chances, which equals thirty-six. I think that the probabilities of getting both dice to show the six dots, would be about once every thirty-six dumps. But let us make it nearly impossible.

Let us use fifty dice and put them in a large cup. What is your guess of how many times you would dump the cup, to get all fifty dice to show the six dots? It doesn't matter that I would think it is impossible. I'm asking if you agree with me or if you think that if the cup which is full of dice was constantly rolled out every thirty seconds for the next hundred years, non-stop, that it could happen? The Laws of Probabilities is either zero or miraculously rigged according to my opinion, which doesn't count. Your idea is what matters here. But let us not stop at fifty.

How about taking a cheaper Swiss watch that only has about one hundred and fifty pieces. There are much more complex watches that have up to four hundred pieces. But we will use a simpler watch and take it totally apart. All the handles, numbers, glass, metal covers, and springs gets taken apart. Every pin is put in the cup with all the other individual parts. Do not leave a single part assembled with another part. Then with the entire Swiss watch in the cup, shake it, and then dump it on the table. How many times would you have to shake and dump the cup before the fully assembled watch would land on the table? Are you claiming an impossibility? Remember that it has all the parts in the cup. There are no parts missing.

What if it was taken over by a million other people that would continue shaking and dumping the cup for the next million years? Would it ever fall out of the cup fully assembled? Does it absolutely take a designer, a watch smith, to assemble it? Or can 150 pieces fall together by chance in a million years. Once again, we must consult the Laws of Probabilities, and try making it work overtime. Let us increase the complexity.

The human body has about 206 bones. Put all those bones, disassembled, into a barrel. Shake the barrel and dump them out like dice. How many times would you have to shake and dump out those bones before a complete and perfect skeleton would fall out? Yahtze? Maybe in one hundred years, out falls a skeleton that is fairly complete with most of the bones in the right place. However, the skull is not on top of the backbone, but is lodged tight in the pelvic bone! A person could assume it is a missing link-of the modern day politician, maybe?

But on a serious note, there are people that believe this very extreme occurrence actually happened. They believe the barrel of bones is not even necessary. Supposedly each single bone just miraculously formed itself perfectly, to the right specs, out of the mud! Then all 206 bones attached themselves together in the correct place! A finger bone didn't trade places with the femur. All by chance but with perfect order. And yet that is only the skeleton. What about accidentally routing the intestines through the cranium before exiting out the ear canal? This idea makes a person consider if some judges were victims of that mistake by the filthy decisions they make! Seriously that gut mistake through the skull never happens. The brain is locked inside the cranium which I heard has a bone strength when compared equally with the same pounds is stronger than steel!

The many organs are all placed where they are best designed for. Can you tell me how a single cell from a mother, and a single cell from a father, can multiply the cells until it is a masterpiece of design? When the cells start dividing and multiplying, why do cell structures change? One cell divides and becomes hard and hollow, which becomes a specific bone in the proper location? Another cell starts forming thousands of tiny sacks in two large sacks, which are the lungs. Each new cell changes shape, texture, size, and color to make a specific organ.

How do the arteries form to get smaller the further they are from the heart? There still wouldn't be any life if these pipe lines became a dead end. Every single cell has to receive blood, and then have another piping system to take the blood back to the heart. We have a complex body. How can anyone say that it is impossible to dump out 150 separate Swiss watch parts out of a cup, and expect to have an assembled fine running watch dumped onto the table, but then believe our complex body was done without a designer?

If someone went to the doctor for a checkup, and were given the bad news that they had a serious and deadly disease, would the person's opinion matter? They feel good and therefore they don't think the doctor is correct? Not believing something, does that make the disease go away? Not believing in a creator, a heaven, nor a hell; does that totally remove the possibility of being true? Doesn't everyone have faith of either choice? One person must have faith believing something that can't be tested by true science, that out of chaos, perfection came about by chance? Isn't that belief based on a theory of men, and therefore a faith that they are correct? If that theory of men is wrong, what will happen to the people that had faith in it?

Isn't it ironic how someone can believe 37 trillion cells with totally different structures, all just fell together in a perfect masterpiece by chance? But when they throw out fifty million years to this impossibility, now they not only think it's possible, but now they claim it is science! If you read to a child the story of a beautiful girl kissing a toad, and the toad turns into a Prince, they call it a Fairy Tale. But if you add a million years after the kiss you can now claim it as fact and science. Each reader must make a decision what the Laws of Probabilities are if you put 37 trillion cells into a barrel and end up with an awesome body after dumping it out. Do you believe in chance or do you believe that there could be a designer, who is called God? Do you still think our body fell into place by chance. However, if you believe that there must be a designer, a creator, called God, then continue reading. This book might give you ideas or thoughts to ponder on which will eventually get you to enjoy heaven.

Chapter Three

Which Religion?

F or thousands of years, people have worshiped many gods or beliefs. If I start naming them, starting from ancient times, this book would be extensively long. Also if I miss a single one, and not mention it, there would be ill feelings from those followers. So I will just start with the religion that had the greatest impact. As this book is going to print, the year is 2025. What is the description of the year if we add one year onto the present year, and then ask, "What year was it, 2026 years ago?" The answer would be, 1 B.C. What does that mean? Those letters stand for, "Before Christ". Today the numbers increase with each passing year going forward. However, starting at the beginning of that B.C. Switch, the numbers increase going backwards in time. Example is, "What year was it, 3025 years ago?" It was, 1000 B.C. Why should this paragraph be so important?

Jesus Christ made such an impact on everything, including our calendar. No other leader of a religion made such a drastic change. Not even close! After Jesus was killed, segments of a book by his followers were written. People of those days had a certain idea or belief system that was contrary to what this radical man, Jesus, was teaching to be true. The religious people and the politicians of that day both hated what was taught by this man. Therefore they had to kill him in a way or method that would silence him forever, and strike fear into any of his followers. I'm convinced you know the story, because a prominent book was written about the entire event. That book is the Bible. So, for the people who do not know much about that book, "what is in this Bible?"

The contents of that book is actually 66 books put into one book. Over half the books were written before Jesus Christ was born, which is called the Old Testament. The remaining books were written after he was killed, which is called the New Testament. So if you are totally unfamiliar with the Bible, and want to find out how Jesus lived or what he did, read the first four books of the New Testament.

Now, I already mentioned that the authorities had to silence this man and his followers. So they killed Jesus with an extremely painful and torturous death, and Jesus's followers fled the scene during this time. Then something happened that has never happened before or since by any leader from any religious group. No leader can equal what Jesus did next. He was totally dead on that gruesome day. He basically suffocated to death when he was nailed and hung on the cross for hours. Then, after it appeared he was dead, a soldier thrust a spear into Jesus's side which caused water and blood to pour out. But now the best part is about to begin. Jesus was placed in a tomb. Imagine a body placed into a casket and buried underground. Here the difference is, instead of going down, the grave is sideways into a hillside. Roman soldiers are keeping guard to ensure that nobody steals this dead body.

Then, on the third day it happened! Jesus came back to life! No dead religious leader has ever done that before. Anyone that saw him, and then dared to tell anyone about it could be killed. So here is the spoiler alert. Thousands of people died because they saw, they believed, they told others, and then were killed also. Peter was one man that walked with Jesus for about three years before Jesus was nailed to a cross. Peter saw Jesus after he came back to life, and talked about it wherever he went. The authorities had to silence him and started to nail him to the cross. Peter pleaded that he is not worthy to be crucified in the same way that his Lord and Savior, Jesus Christ had died. Therefore, Peter died crucified like Jesus, except upside down.

Paul was another prominent man. In the beginning he was one of the leaders in authority, and had killed many of the Christ followers. Read the fifth book, Acts, of the New Testament in the Bible, to see how Paul became a follower of this Jesus movement. His head was chopped off because he declared to everyone that Jesus was alive! If Peter, Paul, or even you, knew that you just made up a story about Jesus being alive, would anyone risk being put to death, knowing that your story is a lie? Their willingness to even die a cruel death happened only because they knew what they experienced was absolutely true. Let us continue by exposing how successful (or not) these religious leaders and authorities were in silencing this radical Jesus teaching.

To be on the New York's Best sellers list, the book has to sell 5,000 to 10,000 copies in a week, which depends on your competition. Let us assume that you have a best seller and it sold 25,000 copies. Now go to the ocean, which we will call sea level. Place one of your fingers on top of the water. Assume the thickness of your finger represents the distance of 25,000. The task I'm giving you next is the effort you need to put forth to go against your number one competitor. Mount Denali is the tallest mountain in North America. It is just over 20,000 feet.

The Holy Bible has sold an estimated 5 to 7 Billion copies. By far it is the best selling book of all time. Let us use the middle estimate of 6 Billion and divide it by your finger thickness which represents 25,000. Now you put one finger on top of the next and repeat until you reach the top of Mount Denali! Climb that mountain by alternating your right and left pointer finger on top of each other as you struggle to the top. When you have reached the summit, you have finally caught up with the greatest competitor that has no runner up, not even close enough to challenge the title.

Summarize this chapter. Jesus drastically changed

our calendar, which dictates what year it is, recent history or thousands of years ago. History proves not only by the calendar but also many artifacts or documents that Jesus lived. There are also confirmations that Jesus was killed, crucified. Next, Jesus rose or should we use modern day terms, that he came back to life again. Many people saw and witnessed that he came back to life, and those people didn't deny that truth even onto death. Thousands of people died to confirm the truth that Jesus must be alive. And the story of the Life and Death of this man is recorded, "in this mountain high book sales"!

Most other religions can take you to a grave or tomb and show the remains of their leader. They are still dead. Jesus' tomb was empty. Both the Roman guards and Jesus' followers both witnessed and saw that it was empty. If the soldiers had hidden the body, they could have easily presented it if the followers tried starting a rumor that Jesus is alive. If the followers took the body and hid it to start the rumor that Jesus has risen and is alive, would they have been willing to die for their scam or hoax?

Now it is your turn to decide if Jesus lived, if he died, or if the documentation of this story which is the Bible, should seriously be regarded or considered. If something interested you in this chapter, please continue in your search for truth and your specific "road map" to heaven. Eternity is way too long for your "road map" to be wrong.

Chapter Four

Four Witnesses

I had four children that were old enough to tattle on me. I also had another one that was with mommy in the bedroom getting fed. An object lesson occurred to me which I thought would be fun. At the time of this story, they were still making cassette players which dates this story around the late 1990's. I took a player into the bedroom and gave it to mommy, letting her know what my intentions were. She agreed to the excitement that was bound to happen.

In the living room were my four children and I told them all to quickly sit down. "Mommy is in the bedroom", I said, "and she doesn't know what is going on out here." Mommy has told them that nobody jumps on the couch, but immediately I violated that and bounce a few times. My children were shocked at what they were witnessing. Once off the couch, I removed the cushions and threw them on the floor, and then jumped on them. There was a glass of water standing on the table, so I thrust my hands into that glass getting my hands wet, and then softly slapped my wet hands into a couple of my children's faces. They laughed at what was happening! They never saw their daddy go bananas like that. The table lamp that was on the coffee table was quickly, but carefully, placed on the floor. I don't remember if the table went upside down also.

It was total chaos for a few minutes and the living room looked like a mess! The children were laughing. Then suddenly I faked of being scared. "Oh no! I'm in trouble, mommy is coming", I spoke with urgency. Then, for the next minute, I worked with urgency getting everything put back into place before mommy stepped out of the bedroom. She was told to stay in the bedroom earlier, but the children didn't know that. So now the learning curve was about to happen.

With my children confused by what just happened, but yet enjoying every moment of it, I told my oldest child to go tell mommy what happened. Hesitation was written all over his face not knowing if I meant for him to get me into trouble. I assured him that it was good, that he could tell mommy the truth about what happened in the living room these last five minutes. "Yes, please go tell mommy what I did out here!" After he gave his report to mommy, I sent the second child to tattle on me. Soon all four had their opportunity to tell the story of how daddy went crazy for a few minutes.

Then the surprise came. Mommy came out with the baby, and with the tape recorder! The entire family sat down and the recording was turned on. It was funny how an excited child was out of breath, by just trying to report everything they just saw. Each child gave their version of what happened. None of them told the complete story. All the children put together, might have covered all the bases of what transpired, but each one had missed some of the parts. There was a lot of laughter from everyone, except maybe not from the baby that had been disturbed during its lunch. I said, "All four of you saw the same thing happen, why didn't you all tell the complete story?" "We forgot that part ", they responded.

So now came the revelation to the question they had asked days earlier. Why were there four books in the Bible that are pretty much repeating the same thing? We had read to the children the Gospels which are, Matthew, Mark, Luke, and John. These are the first four books in the New Testament. The light bulb came on in all their little brains. Those four authors of those books all wrote what they remembered, of what they witnessed or heard from their closest friends. They wrote exactly what they knew to be true. And because they experienced it, they didn't deny the truth even though they could be killed for it. And some of the witnesses died telling that awesome truth.

It is reported that Matthew died by the sword. Mark had a rope placed around his neck and drug throughout the streets until he was dead. Luke had his head chopped off and his body thrown into the sea. History is a little uncertain about John's death, but he might have miraculously escaped becoming a boiling oil martyr. It might have been an embarrassment to the ruler that tried to kill him, so John was banished to a tiny island. There he wrote the last book of the Bible, Revelation of Jesus Christ. The consensus is that he finally died of natural causes at the age of ninety.

Now comes your turn. What will you do with the Gospels? Will you believe what those four men wrote? They yielded their security of life to tell you their experience. Would you be willing to be tortured to death for a story that isn't true? They didn't just tell a story that wouldn't have consequences, but they shared an experience that hinged on eternal destinations for everyone in the world. They were willing to die for it. Is it important enough for you to at least read what they experienced? Believing their experienced testimony might provide you a "road map" to heaven with a little more accuracy. I know it will, but that's my opinion.

Chapter Five

Witnesses of Truth

Those four people that saw Jesus, and witnessed what he did, wrote about it. They not only wrote about what they saw and heard, but also were willing to die for what they wrote to be true. There were hundreds of other people that saw the miracles. Read Matthew, Mark, Luke, and John, and study for yourself the harmony among the four authors. Each witnessed that Jesus was credible and that he spoke the truth always. Not once was he proven wrong, nor was there a task of a miracle that didn't work for him.

A wedding was underway and an emergency happened because of poor planning or oversight. There was a shortage of beverage. Jesus did his first miracle. He didn't hope or wish his procedure would work. He ordered the vessels to be filled with water. Then with definite truth of his word, the miracle wine was served to the wedding party. He spake and it happened.

Read about all the different people he healed. He told a crippled lame man to pick up his bed and walk. Was Jesus truthful in notifying the man (in that fashion) that he was healed? Blind people received their sight when Jesus spoke. In Matthew chapter 9, a young maid had died. People were crying and Jesus gave a new definition to sleeping because the creator was present. Jesus said she was sleeping, even though she was dead according to normal human thinking. What happened? Jesus spoke the truth.

There was a strange woman at the well that didn't know Jesus. Please read that story how things developed in John chapter 4. Jesus asked her about her husband, and she responded that she didn't have a husband. Once again the secret hidden truth was spoken that she had five previous husbands and was now living with another man. How would Jesus know that information about a stranger? How about when Jesus spoke the truth about Nathanael being under the fig tree, which that new disciple thought nobody knew about? That story is in John chapter one.

Jesus already knew ahead of time how he was to die. He spoke about it several times throughout his three year ministry to his followers. He told them that he would be killed by the authorities. All his followers would flee away from him when his "court procedures" began. Peter declared that he would stay by his side, even if it meant death. However, Peter fled the scene after the rooster crowed three times, exactly like Jesus said it would happen. Jesus always told the truth, but Peter did not. Jesus also told his disciples that he would be dead in a tomb for three days, but then rise again immediately after that. Jesus spoke the truth again, because it happened just like that.

This Jesus spoke the truth the entire time. Evil people tried framing him with a lie when Jesus said, "Tear this temple down and in three days I will build it back up!" Those evil accusers assumed he was talking about the temple made with timbers and stone. But Jesus was referring to himself, which he did raise back up on the third day after being dead in the tomb for that period. His truth speaking voice calmed the stormy seas. It healed the lame, the sick, the deaf, the blind, and raised the dead. Name another religion whose leader who had that same power to do miracles like this. Can you name a leader of some different religion like that?

There is a belief going around that claims that all the god (small "g") believing people in the world are all serving the same God. They say that everyone that serves some god, is actually going to heaven, just like a Jesus believing person. Does that harmonize with what Jesus said? In John 14:6, Jesus made a claim that is very controversial. ***"I am the way, the truth, and the life: no man cometh unto the Father, but by me."*** He claimed he was the Son of God, and did all those miracles which would have been impossible if God had not been present. He had spoken the truth so many times and now he makes a statement like that? Did he lie this time, or is it true what he just spoke? Every person has to decide that for themselves.

Another passage in scripture is either ignored, minimized, or hated in Matthew 7:21-23. ***"Not every one that saith unto me, Lord, Lord, shall enter into*** *the kingdom of heaven; but he that doeth the will of my Father which is in heaven. Many will say to me in that day, Lord, Lord, have we not prophesied in thy name? And in thy name have cast out devils? And in thy name done many wonderful works? And then will I profess unto them, I never knew you: depart from me, ye that work iniquity.* " Why would Jesus make such a chilling comment? Doesn't it sound like it's talking about people that are religious, to say the least? It sounds like they are casting out devils and doing possibly some miracles. But then why does he condemn them to hell? What is missing? This same Jesus that spoke the truth these three years with all the healing miracles, and feeding thousands of people with two small fish,....is he now speaking untruth? If he is speaking the truth, it should scare everyone enough to search what he meant by the last two paragraphs of this book.

In the remainder of this book, let us try to figure out what he meant by these statements. Our "road map" for Eternity hangs in limbo until we can figure out what Jesus meant. I may not be able to give you the answer, but I will try to give you enough scripture pertaining to this topic, so you can make the most serious decision of your life.

Chapter Six

Opposite Bookends

The Old Testament of the Bible was written in Hebrew, while the New Testament was written in Greek. Most people that are reading the Bible, do not know either of those languages. Someone, or several people had to translate it from those languages into English so you and I could understand what was written. Unfortunately, sometimes in translation, the thought of what was written in Greek or Hebrew, was wrongfully put into English words and, therefore, incorrect. To defend the translation into English, very minor details are wrong or confusing of what was meant. The confusing part is when two verses or extensive thoughts contradict each other. Someone coined the idea that they are Opposites, like opposite bookends. They consider that one idea could be the left bookend, and the other thought the right bookend. Which side is the correct interpretation?

I hope you have noticed that when it is a scripture that I am typing for this book, I will use **BOLD and *Italics.*** As examples of opposite bookends, we will start with Proverbs 26:4. ***Answer not a fool according to his folly, lest thou also be like unto him.*** However, the very next verse, number 5, says just the opposite! ***Answer a fool according to his folly, lest he be wise in his own conceit.*** Opposites! Somewhere in translating something went wrong. Could there be differences in what type of fool? The fool in verse 5 could be a foolish one that might just be ignorant, and claiming something that you could easily show or prove that his idea is wrong? Could the other fool of verse 4, be a belligerent fool that argues like a drunk? He rambles on about something that is so far off from truth, but that fool will continue arguing that you are wrong. Advice from that scripture, don't respond to him. Walk away from him is also a good practice.

I think of something that happened to me several years ago. I heard of two men that were canoeing down a river that they didn't know. It might have been in the 1800's. Anyway, as they floated down this river the momentum started to increase rapidly. They were in the middle of the river when they looked up ahead to see what was causing this river to increase speed. They saw a few hundred yards ahead, the horrific situation they were in. They not only saw it, but could now hear the roar of a huge waterfall! There was one large boulder in the middle of the river just in front of them. The river at this point was moving way too fast to get to either shore. They barely caught this rock in the river and hung on for dear life! If their fingers slipped and they let go of that rock, they will go over the falls in the next few moments and die.

All night long they had to hang on with all their strength knowing their fate if they didn't. To them it must have seemed like years for daylight and the morning to come. When it finally arrived, it was a miracle to them that someone noticed them and the rescue was in progress. They were rescued, but the part that intrigued me most is the fact that their hair had changed color. Just hours earlier they had dark hair, or whatever hair color they had for years. However, under the extreme stress of the overnight hours, their hair had turned to gray. When I heard that story I believed that it was true. In Proverbs 14: 15, it says a simple minded person is gullible and believes anything that someone tells them, but a wise person will check it out and verify if it is true.

At this point I was the simple minded person, or like the ignorant fool that doesn't know any better, since I hadn't verified if this story could be true. So impressed with the story, I told it to a group of people. They laughed at me for being so gullible. They told me that hair is basically dead, and it grows from the roots. They didn't grow gray hair several inches long overnight. Confused I walked away from that group, thinking that I was caught up in believing something that is impossible.

I talked to a beautician about how hair grows white. Here is a person that cuts hair about forty hours a week. She told me in all her years of cutting hair, she has never found a hair that was a dark color half way out to the end of that hair, and white hair coming from the roots. She told me every hair is either the original natural color, or it is gray. No hair is half of each color.

After that I talked to another older man about that waterfall story. He told me that it could definitely be a true story. He told me his older sister, in her senior citizen years, had open heart surgery a few years earlier. She went into surgery with dark colored hair. Because of the intense stress of the surgery, when she woke up in the recovery room several hours later, she had a totally gray head of hair. Therefore, that man told me that he could believe that story to be true. I had been challenged for possibly being the ignorant fool that babbles out nonsense, but I searched the matter out to verify if this waterfall story could possibly be a true event. The science, or the human anatomy incidents made this story possible.

But let me tell you another story of when I acted (as in pretending) the part of a fool. I did this acting to challenge my children to practice their debate skills. I told them that back when Jesus was born, the feeder boxes which the animals ate out, were called mangers. These mangers were the size of king size beds because when the shepherds came, they found the entire family bedded down in the manger. ***And they came with haste, and found Mary, and Joseph, and the babe lying in a manger.*** Luke 2:16 My children argued with me that it said the babe was lying in the manger. I resisted and asked them what the word "and" meant? Did it not mean, "including" Mary, including Joseph, including the babe; ALL three included – lying in the manger?

We had fun debating this issue. If I had not acted, but actually believed this nonsense, I would be a fool. Depending on how hard I argued, or if there was no one that could change my mind, that would determine what type of fool I was. Don't walk away from me, instead RUN!

Another often used "bookend" is the verse a person hears when the person that is offended at what you said, and responds to you with, "You shouldn't judge!" ***Judge not, that ye be not judged, For with what judgment ye judge, ye shall be judged: and with what measure ye mete, it shall be measured to you again.*** Matthew 7:1-2. Usually only the first seven words get used for this "Left side" bookend. Before we try to explain that verse, let us read another verse that Jesus said also, which could be the opposite, as in "Right side" bookend. ***Judge not according to the appearance, but judge righteous judgment.*** John 7:24 How can we fit between these two opposite bookends?

Doesn't the word judge have several meanings? You get ready to cross the street and see a car a few hundred yards away coming toward you. You absolutely must "judge" if it is safe to cross the street at this time. Do you "judge" the speed and distance of that approaching car? You get ready to prepare a meal or a meeting somewhere for a gathering. What kind of disaster could happen if you refused to "judge" how many people are coming?

Will you "judge" how much food you need? What happens if you have an appointment somewhere, and you refuse to "judge" what time you need to leave to make that appointment?

There is a man coming toward you swinging a baseball bat. He is glaring at you and cursing as he is approaching. Will you "judge" him as to what his intentions are? Or will you try to repeat the first seven words of "you shouldn't judge" and just stand there? Suddenly with those thoughts or questions, the opposite bookends come closer together. Suppose you saw somebody you love dressed up as the devil. They even painted their visible skin red. Suppose you are shocked at their appearance, and ask them if they couldn't have selected a different outfit or character? They then yell in your face, "you shouldn't judge! Isn't that in the Bible, you self righteous hypocrite?" What if you asked them, "Are you judging me, that I'm judging you?"

There is a judgment that is wrong to do. God decides who goes to heaven and hell. It would be wrong to say, "That person is going to hell." That type of judgment is for Eternity and belongs to God. But let us scrutinize the complete two verses of Matthew 7:1-2. Does it not basically say, that we will be judged in the same way we judge others? There are people that are extremely critical and condemning of everyone around them. Read those two verses and tell me if you could agree that this person will be judged extremely critical by God, because he judged others critically?

Now read Romans 2:21-22 *Thou therefore which teachest another, teachest thou not thyself? Thou that preachest a man should not steal, dost thou steal? Thou that sayest a man should not commit adultery, dost thou commit adultery? Thou that abhorrest idols, dost thou commit sacrilege?* It is about condemning someone else and yet doing equal or worse than they. God might just be more critical to them.

Have you ever heard the expression, "Don't criticize a person, until you have walked a mile in his shoes? I'm glad it said "his" shoes, instead of "her" shoes. I wouldn't walk one hundred yards in high heels, and definitely not a mile. That would definitely be torture equal to water boarding! Continuing with this book, I just hope I can put enough lighter reading stories into this chapter and into the rest of the book, to compensate for this heavy scripture reading. So please just press through these remaining chapters which seem more like a Bible study, and I will try my best to make it interesting. However, the context in the next few chapters will be intense, but your Eternal outlook might hinge on the following content.

Let us dive into another Opposite bookends topic. *That if thou shalt confess with thy mouth the Lord Jesus, and shalt believe in thine heart that God hath raised him from the dead, thou shalt be saved.* Romans 10:9. We will label that the left side, and now let us use a scripture for the opposite right side. *Thou believest that there is one God; thou doest well: the devils also believe, and tremble. But wilt thou know, O vain man, that faith without works is dead?* James 2:19-20. How many people have you heard say that they believe in God? Is that the only requirement to make heaven? The devils also believe and tremble! Does this Jesus believing individual tremble as the devils are? Because the devils also believe, will they go to heaven? Doesn't the "right side" bookend, somehow take away the free spirit type of belief, or at least, become a little weak on requirement? Verse 20 goes right into another Opposite bookend, when it states, "*faith without works is dead*".

Here is the left side bookend. *For by grace are ye saved through faith; and that not of yourselves: it is a gift of God: Not of works, lest any man should boast.* Ephesians 2:9 Now let us look at a right side bookend. *But wilt thou know, O vain man, that faith without works is dead?* (verse 20) James 2:14-26. Elon Musk is supposed to be the richest man on earth, with a net worth of $343 billion dollars! Suppose there is a race that every human has to enter. The object of that race is not to be first at crossing the finish line. Instead, if you cross the finish line with your best efforts, you receive Eternal riches. If you don't run that race, you get Eternal disaster. The cost however, to enter that race is ten Trillion dollars! Even Mr. Musk can't afford the ticket to get in for that race.

To shorten the explanation of the impossibility of entering this race because of the outrageous cost, (spoiler alert!) Jesus paid for it on the cross for all of us. (Ephesians 2:9) Ask Jesus for that entrance to the race ticket which he is handing out to anyone that wants it! But now after you receive that ticket, it is our duty to work at this race, to put effort forth to cross that finish line victoriously. (James 2:14-26). Do you think a person just can "enjoy" sin and expect to make heaven without effort or to say "no" to the evil sins? That question leads to another set of bookends in a later chapter. Are there differences or degrees in sin? But first, turn on your imagination skills and bake a pie with me.

Chapter Seven

An Exotic Triple Pie

L et's make a pie that you may never forget. Please get a special pie pan that has three compartments, for three different pies. I want two of the compartments the same size and that they each use up almost half of the pie. I need each of the two big sections to give just a little sliver to the third type of pie. Do you follow me so far with two large areas and one tiny?

We will make the tiny pie first so let us gather the ingredients for it. Go get a cup of the black berries from the nightshade plant- Atropa belladonna. Yes, those berries are poisonous and deadly. Symptoms begin about an hour after eating them. Don't run away from this interesting baking class. I am not a murderer in the making. You will soon see the point I will make with this pie. Hang in there, and please follow along.

After you have those berries, you will need to travel to Africa for the next ingredient. In the bush you will search for a special snake. The common size for this type of snake you will need to search for is a six to eight foot long snake with a trophy size of fourteen feet long. You must look for the most common color which is gray. But now comes the test. You must make it raise it's head and open it's mouth to prompt it to strike. If you get to that point, check if it has a totally black mouth. If it does, you have done excellent at finding a Black Mamba! The name received is because the color inside it's mouth and not the color of it's skin or scales. I always thought it would be a black snake, but instead it is either gray or brown.

Now you must capture it and suck out every drop of it's poisonous venom. It is one of the most poisonous snakes of the world! Add the venom as the second ingredient to those poisonous berries. Next you must find Black Widow Spiders. Get several of them because you need to collect enough venom which is fifteen times more potent than rattlesnake venom.

Finally you can get the fourth ingredient which is not as dangerous to collect. Find a tame cow and feed her White Snakeroot, which is a weed or flowering grass. After she has eaten a bunch of it, get a cup of milk from her and mix it well with the other three ingredients you have already collected. President Abraham Lincoln's mother died from drinking milk from a cow that had eaten that poisonous plant. Congratulations for gathering all four of those ingredients, and that small sliver part of the third pie is complete. We must now focus on making the other two larger pies.

The second pie is not as exotic, because we will make a special cherry pie, quite different than the usual way of making it. Normally the pit or seed gets taken out and thrown away. However, for this pie we must keep the seed. You can take the flesh part off and set that aside, but collect every seed and then grind them to powder. Add that powder back into the flesh of the cherries which had those seeds taken out. I must now take a break from teaching you how to make these pies, to tell you a true story that happened to me about ten years ago.

I started making fruit shakes daily with a blender. I used a variety of fruits including apples. It is common to eat sunflower seeds, pumpkin seeds, and even grape seed which you can't remove very well. You just eat the grapes and spit out any seeds that are too obnoxious to chew or swallow. Strawberry seeds are on the outside of the fruit. You get the picture by now, that usually the seeds are eaten. Then after removing the core of the apple for several weeks, I decided to change things. I just took the stem off and threw the entire apple into the blender. Lot less work, and this was quicker.

Something happened within one or two weeks. I came down with diarrhea and I started feeling sick. Thinking that it was just a flu and that these symptoms should be gone in a few days, I didn't give it much more thought. I excused the thought that it could be the fruit shakes that I'm drinking, because I had done them for weeks and this sickness just started. After a month I started getting worried. I didn't have insurance to go to the doctor, nor did I have the money to do it. The second month it was even worse. My stomach rumbled constantly and my toilet episodes were a blast of water and done.

By the third month I started to do some research and I don't remember what prompted me in the right direction. Maybe somebody said something that turned on the idea of why this is happening. The answer was alarming when I realized that I was poisoning myself ignorantly with cyanide! I didn't know that if I had increased the dosage of ground apple seeds and lengthened the duration of usage, I could have died soon after that. I was well underway of getting to the mortuary. Apple seeds contain cyanide if they are smashed or ground up. Several other fruits and berries have that poison too, and cherries do also. I never knew that before my near fatal ordeal. But now that I know this, it is the precise reason we are baking almost a half of this pie with the cherry seeds ground up and added back into the ingredients.

Use any recipe for the cherry pie to add the rest of the missing ingredients which I didn't mention. The only requirement for this new exotic pie is to add the ground seeds into it which are poisonous. However, one slice of this pie isn't going to kill you. The time frame it takes for it to kill you is the daily habitual feasting on it for several days, and without any desire to quit eating it. It will kill you eventually if you continue.

And now let us finish the last and third pie. You can choose if it will be lemon or banana cream pie, as long as it is a yellow color. Just use a recipe to get the right ingredients. There probably will be trans fat which is not good for you. Don't forget the sugar which is also hard on your body. You can link a lot of ailments or diseases to this processed food diet. But you can live a normal life for a long time eating this type of pie without having immediate and severe complications like the other two pies in this same pie pan.

Let us bake this triple pie and evaluate each one of them. Do not take even one bite out of the first pie which is smaller than the other two. You will die probably within the hour. There probably is no remedy or medical procedure to keep you alive. Now the cherry pie you might be able to consume for several days, but after eating it a month or two, you better change your eating habit or you will die also. The third yellow pie is normal. It's not good for you, but it isn't deadly like the other two. Sure there will be consequences from eating that. Feeling sluggish, indigestion, gaining weight, and the sickness and discomforts continue with a long list. But usually you can live a long time. I want to thank you for visualizing this baking demonstration or episode of this chapter. The significance of this chapter lies in the rest of the book. I hope I can bring it all together so you will never forget this exotic pie.

Chapter Eight

Are There Different Degrees Of Sin?

These next opposite bookends are probably the most serious, and also the most debated from both sides of understanding. Therefore, you have to really analyze all the scripture on this topic and make your own decision on what is the correct path to take. I will repeat again that I don't want you to accept my interpretation without you intensely studying this topic.

The left bookend is; *All unrighteousness is sin....*1John 5:17. The original definition of "sin", was "missing the mark" of perfection. Suppose a person is under tremendous stress and then someone asks a question that is irritating, and this stressed person lashes out verbally which he later regrets. It was not righteous for him to spew those words out with anger. He had missed the mark of perfection. Is it as bad as the opposite bookend? Jesus spoke these next words; *All manner of sin and blasphemy shall be forgiven unto men: but the blasphemy against the Holy Ghost shall not be forgiven unto men. And whosoever speaketh a word against the Son of man, it shall be forgiven him: but whosoever speaketh against the Holy Ghost, it shall not be forgiven him, neither in this world, neither* *in the world to come.* Matthew 12:31-32

Those two verses just mentioned in Matthew show by themselves, that there are at least two levels of sin. Don't those two verses declare that anyone who blasphemes the Holy Ghost, that it absolutely brings forth eternal death and damnation. It doesn't seem like there is any antidote nor remedy to justify or survive this action. Could you see the similarities with this action, and the action of eating the "night shade pie laced with venom"? You eat that pie and death is inescapable. It's definite that you will die physically eating that pie, and blasphemes against the Holy Ghost you die spiritually, forever! Nothing can keep you alive with either comparison.

But the left bookend which was mentioned two paragraphs earlier, was not the complete verse. *All unrighteousness is sin: and there is a sin not unto death.* Does it admit that a certain sin is permissible or at least excusable? Does it seem that this type of sin may not be good like the lemon pie, but yet it doesn't bring forth eternal death? By now you must think about the Cherry pie, and what is the comparison with it? Is there a sin that is worse than the Lemon pie but not instantaneous death like the venom pie? What about this verse in Revelation? *But the fearful, and unbelieving, and the abominable, and murderers, and whoremongers, and sorcerers, and idolaters, and all liars, shall have their part in the lake which burneth with fire and brimstone: which is the second death.*

Revelation 21:8 Isn't it obvious that the "sin not unto death" is different than this Revelation list? Isn't this list condemning any partakers of these acts to hell? Isn't a partaker of this list somewhat equal to the person eating the Cherry cyanide pie? If the person quits eating this pie physically like I did with the apple seeds, they can live. But if you continue to feast on that pie or that list of hell bound "sins", could you die spiritually?

I can see at least three levels of sin, but the real important point is if you can see it in the last few paragraphs? The left side bookend gets another reinforcement for that side of the argument. ***For whosoever shall keep the whole law, and yet offend in one point, he is guilty of all.*** James 2:10 Do you think that verse could mean that if you missed the mark and spoke harshly to someone, that you are now guilty of blaspheme against the Holy Ghost? Would heaven be empty then of every human being? After all, blasphemes are unpardonable, and so does that make a hasty word unpardonable also? Or could that verse basically include all the ingredients in the Cherry cyanide pie? Could it mean that any of the identities of the Revelation list, could be judged as them having done all of those "sins"? An example of that might be if the person is an unbeliever is he the same as a murderer? Or at least in the same category of murderer? But we still need to see if there really is at least a "triple style pie". What verses and reinforcement can we put on the right side of the argument of degrees of sin?

Jesus was brought to Pilate to be questioned in the process of getting crucified. Pilate feared of what he had heard about Jesus, that he could be the Son of God. He asked Jesus some questions but Jesus remained silent. Then Pilate declared his false belief that he had power, which he didn't possess. Jesus responded truth to him which made Pilate even more afraid. ***Thou couldest have no power at all against me, except it were given thee from above: therefore he that delivered me unto thee hath the greater sin.*** John 19:11 Why would Jesus say anything about a <u>greater sin</u>? Is there a lesser sin? Doesn't it somewhat indicate that there are degrees or severity of "sin", possibly making different judgments pertaining to what sin was committed?

If you have read the four gospels, which are the events which happened during the life of Christ, from four different witnesses, you will have read about the woman caught in sexual misbehavior. The Old Testament law required a woman caught in adultery was to be killed by stoning her to death. Did all the "sins" of that day require death in that fashion? If all the "sins" were regarded equal, would anyone be left alive? In fact, when the woman was brought to Jesus, he somewhat reinforced the left side bookend. ***He that is without sin among you, let him first cast a stone at her.*** John 8:7 Definitely two opposite bookends in the last two verses, or are they opposite?

Did Jesus try to change the Old Testament ways of dealing with this type of "sin"? Instead of being extremely judgmental resulting in instant death on certain "sins", Jesus brought in a new dispensation of forgiveness of sins. But what extremely important words did Jesus tell that woman next? Many are the "Left side arguments", that miss the "right side" of these opposite bookends. Do you know what he said? ***Neither do I condemn thee, go, and sin no more.*** John 8:11 Was it a command or a demand that Jesus gave to the woman? Was she supposed to quit all sin? Did Jesus give her an impossibility? She better not talk harsh to anyone! Or was Jesus talking about not "sinning" by feasting on the cyanide Cherry pie any longer? Paraphrasing what he said, didn't he basically demand that she is supposed to quit adultery and such like?

Jesus spoke these words. ***For I say unto you, That except your righteousness shall exceed the righteousness of the scribes and Pharisees, ye shall in no case enter into the kingdom of heaven.*** Matthew 5:20 The Scribes and Pharisees were the religious leaders in that day. They followed the Law of Moses to the best that they knew how. And yet Jesus compared their righteousness with the righteousness that is required. Doesn't that make degrees about good acts or conduct? If it is a good act, like Jesus stated that these rulers had a "righteousness", was it just an imitation of purity? Was it all a fake performance of "holy"? ***Woe unto you, Scribes and Pharisees, hypocrites! For ye devour widows' houses, and for a pretense make long prayer: therefore ye shall receive the greater damnation.*** Matthew 23:14 If there is a greater damnation, is there also a lesser damnation? Is there a greater and lesser sin also?

Sodom was a very sinful city. God caused fire from heaven to destroy it. But the degree of "sin" committed in that city, was it at a lesser evil than what the city of Capernaum was doing? ***But I say unto you, That it shall be more tolerable for the land of Sodom in the day of judgment, than for thee.*** Matthew 11:24 Doesn't that verse indicate differences in "sin"? Is there a more tolerable and therefore also a less tolerable? And yet in Genesis 18:20, ***And the Lord said, Because the cry of Sodom and Gomorrah is great, and because their sin is very grievous... .*** If God called it very grievous, isn't there a less grievous to balance that word usage? Do you believe that there are different levels of "sin" or degrees? So let us study of how the lemon pie and the cyanide cherry pie could be used as a measurement for comparison.

Chapter Nine

Lemon Pie

Humanity is a weak candidate in many areas of comparison with other animals or plants. A dog is such a loyal and forgiving companion. The owner could accidentally beat his dog, and yet when the owner comes to his senses and realizes his sandwich was not taken by his dog, the dog comes back, total forgiveness. Humans usually hold grudges. Doesn't it usually take a human a lot longer to forgive a wrong that they had to endure?

Let us make up a bunch of Lemon Pie examples. Unforgiveness is one of those Lemon pie attitudes that could be rated as sin. I don't know the correct answer, but would heaven be without anyone that had unresolved "Lemon pie" still on their tongue when they died? Was holding a distance from someone that had wronged them, on the list of hell bound characteristics in Revelation? I didn't see it. Was speaking a hasty harsh word on that Revelation list? I didn't see that one either.

Suppose there was an elderly couple living in your community. Suddenly the wife dies leaving the husband all by himself. He is in deep grief over his loss. Isolation in this lonely house gets to him but he has no where to go to get away from this haunting void now. You notice the need to visit him and to bring him a dish of food. It would be such a blessing to him since his wife had done all the cooking. The company of having someone to talk to would be priceless to him. However, the duties of every day makes it hard to schedule that desire into this busy life. Days go by, and soon weeks have passed also. But your desire to visit that old isolated man is still on your mind and you purpose to do it soon. Several weeks later that old man, heartbroken, dies also! A tidal wave of emotions and regrets flood your soul. "I have failed, I have missed the mark, ***Therefore to him that knoweth to do good, and doeth it not, to him it is sin***. (James 4:17), I have sinned!" The man had died, and the desire of visiting him can never be done anymore. Now is this a hell bound sin? Is it the cherry cyanide pie which you will die for? Or is it an example of the verse in the beginning of the last chapter? 1 John 5:17 ***and there is a sin not unto death***? Is it the Lemon pie that probably isn't good for your body, but it isn't going to kill you?

How about a contractor which goes to a professed Christian house to bid on a job? After the job is started the contractor finds out that there were hidden complications which were atypical. Upon completion of the project, the contractor writes the invoice at thirty percent more than the original bid. The Christian argues with the contractor that he should have known the career he is claiming to represent and only pays him for the original bid which he quoted. The contractor is offended and spreads his opinion of this customer wherever he goes. He also wants nothing to do with religion or any other so called Christians.

As words spread like wild fire, it often returns to whoever was responsible for it. That Christian meets by accident another owner and contractor of the same profession. That contractor had heard of what happened. He explains to this Christian that occasionally he would tear into a wall and find things hidden that nobody could guess before hand. Maybe there was no foundation and the building was just resting on boards that had rotted away. Maybe there was asbestos that increases the cost drastically for the removal of it. The contractor admits if he had gotten the job, he too would be in the same situation. The Christian suddenly realizes that he had done wrong! I have sinned!

But having a misunderstanding of a certain situation of construction cost, is it a Cherry pie -cyanide sin? Ignorantly "cheating" the contractor the thirty percent, is that a "wrong", listed in the list of hell bound "sins"? Just remember that there is, **A SIN NOT UNTO DEATH!** Could it be like a Lemon Pie that has no poison but does have ingredients that are not exactly healthy?

Chapter Ten

Cherry Cyanide Pie

Cyanide is a poison that will eventually kill you. Repentance basically means that the sinner has identified his "sin" and then asked for forgiveness. But it doesn't stop there. True repentance is turning away from, and quit doing that evil deed. To clarify this paragraph is difficult unless an example is given. Let us use the example of adultery as the cyanide seed that was ground up and consumed. A married person has an affair with someone else who is not their spouse. Conviction hits and they seek God for forgiveness. *If we confess our sins, he is faithful and just to forgive us our sins, and to cleanse us from all unrighteousness.*1 John 1:9 God did promise that all sins can be forgiven except blasphemes against the Holy Ghost. And yes, adultery, which is having an outside of marriage affair, can be forgiven.

But the question that is of greater importance is, does the sinner forsake that behavior? Do they eat another piece of that Cherry cyanide pie next week? Do you think it matches the definition of repentance, if they continued eating the same pie? Doing the same sin weekly? When Jesus spoke the words, *Go, and sin* *no more...*did he not basically say in this symbolism, stop eating this poisonous pie? When Philippians 2:12 states, ***work out your own salvation, with fear and trembling***, doesn't the "***work***" require effort or energy of some sort? A beautiful person makes sexual advances towards you. Doesn't it take a lot of effort or "***WORK***" to say NO? It does take a lot of energy when they look so attractive. Some people might argue that even the desire to have that person is already sin. Is that Lemon Pie or Cherry cyanide Pie? To get from the Lemon over to the Cherry is a progression, isn't it?

Let us break a couple verses down to show the progression. First let it flow freely. ***But every man is tempted, when he is drawn away of his own lust, and enticed. Then when lust hath conceived, it bringeth forth sin: and sin, when it is finished, bringeth forth death.*** James 1:14-15 Using King David as an illustration or example, we will dissect the progression of these two verses.

But every man is tempted... We are all humans with natural desires. That is the Lemon Pie of humanity. If this desire were wrong and a "sin unto death", would heaven be empty? Nobody can make it,...unless it is the idea that Jesus covered all sins (except blasphemes) which is true. However, there are verses that need to be addressed before this chapter ends that might cause a problem for that concept. King David had multiple women but yet he had a desire that was not harnessed. He stood on his lofty palace and looked down on the beautiful scenery below! There was Bathsheba taking a bath, and out in the open view! ***Temptation!*** If he would have turned around and walked off his balcony, and back inside his palace, things would have been different.

When he is drawn away of his own lust, and enticed... King David started tasting this Cherry Pie and it was delicious. Any man that would deny that is not honest, or a homosexual. The lust is powerful, and he progressed to the next step of being ***ENTICED***! He wanted her so bad, that he inquired about who she was? She was Uriah's wife!

Then when Lust hath Conceived, it bringeth forth sin..... King David's fork moves from the Lemon Pie, over to the Cherry Pie which was the "Cyanide", the spiral decline to death. Partaking of this sin is deadly. He had an affair. If he had repented at the finish of that act, things could have been slightly different. Death in several ways had already begun.

And sin, when it is finished, bringeth forth death. Bathsheba became pregnant! Oops! When bread rises, leave town? The more effort people employ in hopes of covering up a sin, quite often the worse the problem becomes. King David indirectly killed Uriah. In a short time, he committed adultery and then murder. Death of Uriah! After that, the death of the baby which was born as a result. Up to this point in David's life, God had richly blessed him. Now there was a "death" of those constant peaceful blessings. From that time forward, David was on the run from his own son who wanted to kill him. His life unraveled compared to his previous life before his affair. There was a "death" to that plush living in the palace life style.

Sure God forgave King David, but he reaped the harvest of the flesh for the rest of his life. Too many people do not consider the seriousness of the following two verses. ***Be not deceived; God is not mocked: for whatsoever a man soweth, that shall he also reap. For he that soweth to his flesh shall of the flesh reap corruption; but he that soweth to the Spirit shall of the Spirit reap life everlasting.*** Galatians 6:7-8 Feasting on the Cherry cyanide pie will bring consequences. The argument that God forgives every sin, and the reaping of that sin, will never happen if you ask for forgiveness, could it be a wrong belief? Maybe? We might comprehend it better with another illustration.

A person hangs out in a bar and gets drunk which is a sin. ***Know ye not that the unrighteous shall not inherit the kingdom of God? Be not deceived:....nor drunkards,...shall inherit the kingdom of God.*** Parts of; 1 Corinthians 9-10. After he leaves the bar, he gets in his car and attempts to drive home. He loses control and slams into a tree that simply jumped out in front of him! What an evil tree! It wasn't his fault, he claims. In the process, his car is totaled, his license is taken away, and one of his legs is amputated! If that person repents, does God forgive him? Absolutely, under the correct heart or soul remorse. But the reaping of the sowing to the flesh for that night, continues until the day he dies. He might be able to eventually get his license back. But he will never get that same leg back. He simply feasted on that Cherry cyanide pie!

Do you know the historical meaning of "Running through the gauntlet"? Many years ago, it was a severe form of punishment. Two rows of soldiers were lined up with clubs or weapons. The criminal had to run between and through those two rows, while the soldiers would thrash or beat that criminal as they passed by. There are numerous verses that apply to this Cherry cyanide Pie, and it will seem like an intense Bible study, which is not the motive. The purpose is to put all these verses together which are spread throughout the Bible, to MAGNIFY the cyanide in this pie. It is a warning to pay attention to the danger of this pie. Therefore, these scriptures will be lined up, without much input of thought, until you "Run this Gauntlet" of scriptures.

These verses however, are not your Enemies, but they could be your redemption if you embrace them. Jesus talked about himself as the Chief corner stone. ***And whosoever shall fall on this stone shall be broken: but on whomsoever it shall fall, it will grind him to powder.*** Matthew 21:44 Doesn't it appear that if we surrender to Jesus while we are still living, it is as if we fell on that "stone (Jesus)", and were broken from wanting to do what our flesh desires? But if we still do the things of sin and then physically die, doesn't it suggest that this same stone will grind us to powder? So now, this gauntlet is for your own good, if you consider each verse with extreme seriousness. So fall on these "stones" to get a FULL UNDERSTANDING of the cyanide. Ready? Get Set? Go!

- *But refuse profane and old wive's fables, and exercise <u>thyself rather unto Godliness</u>. 1 Timothy 4:7*

- *Seeing then that all these things shall be dissolved, what manner of persons ought ye to be in all <u>Holy</u> conversation and <u>Godliness</u>. 2 Peter 3:11*

- *That he would grant unto us, that we, being delivered out of the hand of our enemies, might serve him without fear, <u>In Holiness</u> and <u>Righteousness</u> before him, <u>all the days of our life</u>. Luke 1:74-75*

- *Awake to righteousness, <u>AND SIN NOT</u>: for some have not the knowledge of God: I speak this to your shame. 1 Corinthians 15:34*

- *For I say unto you, that except your righteousness shall exceed the righteousness of the scribes and Pharisees, ye shall in no case enter into the kingdom of heaven. Mt. 5:20*

- *Be ye therefore <u>perfect</u>, even as your Father which is <u>perfect</u>. Mt. 5:48*

- *And if the <u>RIGHTEOUS</u> scarcely (barely) be saved, where shall the <u>UNGODLY</u> and the <u>SINNER</u> appear? 1 Peter 4:18* Are you living righteously for God, or do you continuously claim that you are a daily sinner of the Cherry Pie type? The gauntlet continues.

- *Afterward Jesus findeth him in the temple, and said unto him, Behold thou art made whole; <u>SIN NO MORE</u>, lest a worse thing come unto thee. John 5:14*
- Woman caught in adultery. *And Jesus said unto her, Neither do I condemn thee, <u>GO, AND SIN NO MORE.</u> John 8:11*
- *Because it is written, Be ye <u>Holy</u>; for I am <u>Holy</u>. 1 Peter 1:16*
- *But thou, O man of God, flee these things: and follow <u>after RIGHTEOUSNESS, GODLINESS,</u> faith, love, patience, meekness. Titus 6:11*
- *Follow peace with all men, and <u>HOLINESS,</u> without which no man shall see the Lord. Hebrew 12:14*
- *For kings, and for all that are in authority; that WE may lead a quiet and peaceable life <u>IN ALL GODLINESS</u> and honesty. 1 Timothy 2:2*
- *Having therefore these promises, dearly beloved, let us cleanse ourselves from all filthiness of the flesh and spirit: perfecting <u>HOLINESS</u> in the fear of God. 2 Corinthians 7:1*
- *Teaching us that, denying <u>UNGODLINESS</u> and worldly lusts, we should live <u>SOBERLY,</u>*

<u>RIGHTEOUSLY, AND GODLY IN THIS</u>
<u>PRESENT WORLD.</u> *Titus 2:12*

These are just a few verses that begin this quest of what these Cherry Stones are. We need to name or IDENTIFY them to know what we need to fight against. *But the (1) fearful, and (2)unbelieving, and (3)abominable, and (4)murderers, and (5)sorcerers, and (6)idolaters, and all (7)liars, shall have their part in the lake which burneth with fire and brimstone which is the second death. Revelation21:8*

For without are dogs, and (5)sorcerers, and (8) whoremongers, and (4)murderers, and (6)idolaters, and whosoever (9)loveth and maketh (7) a lie. Revelation 22:15

Now the works of the flesh are manifest, which are these; (10) Adultery, (11)fornication, (12) uncleanness, (13)lasciviousness, (6)Idolatry, (14) witchcraft, (15)hatred, (16)variance, (17)emulations, (18)wrath, (19)strife, (20)sedition-s, (21)heresies, (22)envying-s, (4)murderers, (23)drunkenness, (24)revelings, and such like: of the which I tell you before, as I have also told you in time past, <u>THAT THEY WHICH DO SUCH THINGS SHALL NOT INHERIT THE KINGDOM OF GOD.</u> Galatians 5:19-21

So we found basically <u>24 Cherry seeds </u>which we have baked into this cyanide pie. In that list, can you find any of the "sins not onto death" mentioned in the

Lemon Pie category? The 15th stone, "***hatred***", could be questioned. The English word might have a lot of "thunder & Ghost pepper" missing from it, compared to the original translated word, maybe? Could it have the implication of the HATRED Cain had for Abel, and killed him? Do you think that if you added a lot of HOT pepper spice into that word, it could have a much different meaning than strongly disliking something? Back up to the bold and underlined sentence at the last paragraph, is there any exclusion to someone that believes in Jesus? Isn't, ***SHALL NOT***, an absolute? Many people and churches believe and preach differently. Maybe there is a different Bible translation that washes the absolute away?

Chapter Eleven

Revised Version vs. the Re~hearsed Version?

As mentioned before, the Old Testament was written in Hebrew, and the New Testament in Greek. Over four hundred years ago, King James VI of England made a dramatic decision to translate the Ancient writings into the English language of that time. From 1604 to 1611AD, 47 scholars were paid to translate the Hebrew and Greek, which became known as the King James Bible (KJV). Sure, they spoke a funny dialect using words like, "thy" and "thou". So now, if THOU hast a problem with that dialect, THOU couldest go over to THY alternative version, the Revised Standard Version (RSV). That Bible was not written from the ancient languages, but was simply a rewritten version of the KJV bible. They removed the two huge cotton swabs out of the mouth, and spoke modern day vocabulary. The (RSV) is a good Bible.

Now we must explain the Re**hearse**d Version. Before 2025 this Version never existed. There is no version like that because I just made it up at the beginning of this chapter. It is simply a play on words. A **hearse** was first a carriage used to haul a deceased person to the cemetery, and was pulled by horses. Then eventually they turned into automobiles which hauled the dead away. So basically, the Rehearsed Version is to transport death! Could that (made up) translation be Spirit filled, or from God? No! Ironically, could some people actually use this fictitious Version without realizing what they are doing? You can decide that for yourself after some examples are given.

For all __HAVE__ sinned, and come short of the glory of God: Romans 3:23 That is from the KJV, and the word HAVE sounds like past tense, doesn't it? It is true, every human has sinned, and that includes the Cherry Pie sins of hatred or strife, which leads to death. But the Rehearsed Version must read something like this, "For all are sinning, and are daily sinners, and come short of the Glory of God." Do they admit that they daily Feast on the Cherry Cyanide Pie? *And if the __Righteous__ scarcely be saved, where shall the __Ungodly__ and the __SINNER__ appear?* 1 Peter 4:18 Why would anyone want to categorize themselves into the group that will not make heaven?

For God so loved the world, that he gave his only begotten Son, that whosoever believeth in him should not perish, but have everlasting life. John 3:16 The Rehearsed Version basically allows the vast majority to go to heaven. Nearly everyone believes in God. Almost every human that ever lived, has thought or believed there was a higher power, called God. Therefore, everyone will be in heaven?

But God commendeth his love toward us, in that while we __WERE__ yet sinners, Christ died for us. Romans 5:8 Once again, is not that past tense? But the Rehearsed Version claims, while we still are sinners, Christ died for us.

For the wages (payment due) *of sin is death: but the gift of God is eternal life through Jesus Christ our Lord. Romans 6:23* The KJV claims that each week, day, or moment we get a payment for what we have done. We get paid death wages if we sin? Isn't that what it reads? However, the Rehearsed Version doesn't get a paycheck for sinning? Everyone just simply sins, and Jesus must be crucified afresh every day?

Therefore leaving the principles of the doctrine of Christ, let us go on unto __perfection__; not laying again the foundation of repentance from dead works...For it is impossible for those who were once enlightened, and have tasted of the heavenly gift, and were made partakers of the Holy Ghost, And have tasted the good word of God, and the powers of the world to come, If they shall fall away, to renew them again unto repentance; seeing __they crucify to themselves the Son of God afresh, and put him to an open shame.__ Hebrews 6:1,4-6 Does the Rehearsed Version with their translation of daily sinning, and Feasting on the cyanide Pie every day, crucify Jesus afresh every day? According to the KJV passage just typed, is it mandatory to "*go on unto perfection*"? Is it correct to say that the

Rehearsed Version states that nobody is perfect? Please run through the gauntlet again, to see if perfection was a requirement. Isn't the "Perfection" basically talking about the striving towards the eradication of the 24 Cherry Pie stones? It is "work" but not impossible, or is it?

If it is an impossible task of eliminating all those stones, which stone <u>OR SIN</u> is impossible to not commit? Hypothetical: "Sorry! I was just minding my own business, and before I knew it, I accidentally got a beautiful woman pregnant!" How could that have happened without deliberate steps like King David had? Is the Cherry cyanide Pie, basically a willful transgression against God? Isn't the Lemon Pie different in that it was instantaneous? Without notice? A police officer asks a driver who they pulled over a question. In a split second, are they confronted with the idea of telling the truth and incriminating themselves, or telling a lie in hopes of getting out of this jam? Do they choose to Feast on the Poisoned Pie and tell a lie? In the Revelation list, all liars will go to the fire and brimstone, if unrepentant. According to the gauntlet, and the other scriptures presented so far, there will be reaping of which seed they sow at that moment, maybe for Eternity.

Enter ye in at the strait gate; for wide is the gate, and broad is the way that leadeth to destruction, and <u>MANY</u> there be which go in thereat; Because strait is the gate, and narrow is the way which leadeth unto

life, and __FEW__ there be that find it. Matthew 7:13-14 Jesus spoke those words possibly in the Aramaic language. Couldn't this scripture be paralleled to percentages? If there were a hundred apples and someone told you that you could take a FEW, how many would that mean? Maybe five? How about ten? Would twenty apples be a greedy- quite a few? On the flip side, would many and most be closer to the same? If they told you that they accidentally dropped the bushel basket, and MANY of the apples dumped out, how many would you surmise fell on the dirty ground? Maybe at least seventy of them? They didn't say almost all the apples dumped which could possibly mean ninety-five of them?

In the first chapter it was mentioned that almost at all funerals, the comment gets made, "Well, they are in a better place now!" What is wrong with the laws of average, when Jesus spoke the words of MANY and FEW? *Not everyone that saith unto me, Lord, Lord, shall enter into the kingdom of heaven; but he that doeth the will of my Father which is in heaven. Matthew 7:21* Which stones of the 24; of hatred, envying, strife, murder, and adultery is "*doing the will of my Father*"? But the scripture continues*: MANY will say to me in that day, Lord, Lord, have we not prophesied in thy name? And in thy name have cast out devils? And in thy name done many wonderful works? And then will I profess unto them, I never knew you; depart from me, ye that work iniquity. Matthew 7:22-23*

What does the Rehearsed Version change to make this passage acceptable? Doesn't it sound like these individuals were at least very religious? Doesn't it sound like they were doing work for God? So where is the secret ingredient that caused them to be cast away? Could it be the word, "iniquity"? That word means sin.

They that work sin! Are we talking Lemon Pie sin? Or are we talking about the Cherry cyanide pie sin where certain scriptures stated that these will NOT ENTER into the kingdom of heaven. How is your "Road Map" based on scriptures developing? But there is a Rehearsed version choice of scriptures. *There is none righteous, no, not one. Romans 3:12* For the KJV it is true also. = "*For ALL have sinned...*", therefore if you remove the "Landmark" of when a person accepted Jesus Christ into their life, and go back to their birth,... none is righteous. Doesn't the righteousness begin only after salvation and the "work" begins at refusing to Feast on any of the 24 cyanide seeds? But there is one more LONG passage of scriptures that the Rehearsed Version wants to use, except out of context. They do not finish the entire line of thought, but quit before the question, or the response answer to the problem or issue addressed after that. It starts in Romans 7 and continues into Romans 8, but they stop before that. So let us address the problem, then listen to the question, and finish with the solution.

For we know that the law is spiritual: but I am carnal, sold under sin. For that which I do I allow not: for what I would, that do I not; but what I hate, that do I. If then I do that which I would not, I consent unto the law that it is good. Now then it is no more I that do it, but sin that dwelleth in me. For I know that in me (that is, in my flesh,) dwelleth no good thing: for to will is present with me; but how to perform that which is good I find not, For the good that I would I do not: but the evil which I would not, that I do. Now if I do that I would not, it is no more I that do it, but sin that dwelleth in me. I find then a law, that, when I would do good, evil is present with me. For I delight in the law of God after the inward man: But I see another law in my members, warring against the law of my mind, and bringing me into captivity to the law of sin which is in my members.

Could the next question, and then the solution to this problem be missing in the Rehearsed Version? Why have sermons been preached on the above several verses, but then the next bunch of verses avoided or ignored? The extremely Eternal question comes next!

O wretched man that I am! <u>Who shall deliver me from the body of this death?</u> Now comes the answer that is eliminated or avoided in the Rehearsed Version. The next several verses is the SOLUTION to the Cherry cyanide pie problem!

<u>I thank God through Jesus Christ our Lord. So then with the mind I myself serve the law of God; but with the flesh the law of sin. There is therefore now no condemnation to them which are in Christ Jesus,</u>

*who walk <u>NOT after the flesh, but after the Spirit.</u>
For the law of the Spirit of life in Christ Jesus hath
made me free from the law of sin and death. For what
the law could not do, in that it was weak through
the flesh, God sending his own Son in the likeness of
sinful flesh* (Lemon Pie?) *, and for sin, condemned sin
in the flesh: That the righteousness of the law might
be fulfilled in us, who walk not after the flesh, but
after the Spirit. For they that are after the flesh do
mind the things of the flesh; but they that are after
the Spirit the things of the Spirit. For to be carnally
minded is death; but to be spiritually minded is
life and peace. Because the carnal mind is enmity
against God: for it is not subject to the law of God,
neither indeed can be. <u>So then they that are in the
flesh cannot please God.</u> But ye are not in the flesh,
but in the Spirit, if so be that the Spirit of God dwell
in you. <u>Now if any man have not the Spirit of Christ,
he is none of his.</u> And if Christ be in you, the body is
dead because of sin; but the Spirit is life because of
<u>righteousness.</u> But if the Spirit of him that raised up
Jesus from the dead dwell in you, he that raised up
Christ from the dead shall also quicken your mortal
bodies by his Spirit that dwelleth in you. Therefore,
brethren, we are debtors, not to the flesh, to live after
the flesh. For if ye live after the flesh, ye shall die: but if
ye through the Spirit do mortify* (mortify = mortician,
to embalm- to prep it for burial, 24seeds?) *the deeds
of the body, ye shall live. For as many as are led by*

the Spirit of God, they are the sons of God. Romans (from) 7:14, (through) 8:14

I'm sorry for having made you run through this gauntlet of heavy reading, but I will not apologize for the scriptures which was necessary to complete the entire line of thought. After the entire thought is presented, does the Rehearsed Version have the substance to proclaim that we must "sin" every day? Unless, they are referring to the Lemon Pie, which is humanity? Jesus was our high priest. *For we have not an high priest which cannot be touched with the feeling of our infirmities; but was in all points tempted like as we are, yet without sin. Hebrews 4:15* Couldn't the Humanity with the ever present feelings and desires of it, be the Lemon Pie? According to that verse, doesn't it seem like Jesus even had desires like ours but never yielded to the Cherry Pie? How would you dissect or evaluate that scripture? The Rehearsed Version would love to throw the Lemon Pie into the equation of Sins onto death, in order to build a belief that everyone is still a sinner. Jesus must be crucified afresh constantly to pay for a life of sin from us, without any consequences? Nearing the end of this book, have you developed a custom-made "Road map" for yourself, which harmonizes with all the scriptures presented? If you have, I am happy and overjoyed that you can run this race to eternity without Feasting on the Poisoned Pie.

Chapter Twelve

Luke's Final Court Hearing

STATE OF ETERNITY – JURISDICTION OF HUMANITY

HONORABLE PRESIDING JUDGE – GOD

DOCUMENTS USED FOR LAW &

STATUTES – HOLY BIBLE

PROSECUTING ATTORNEY – HOLY SPIRIT

   vs.

DEFENDANT-- Mr. Luke Wahrm

DEFENSE ATTORNEY – Pastor, D.C.Vehr

C OMES NOW, the Defendant, Mr. Luke Wahrm, with his Defense Attorney, his Pastor, D.C.Vehr. He is brought to this court to arrive at a judgment of whether he is guilty of the accusations of his crimes done against the Laws & Statutes of this Eternal Province. If he is found guilty with a preponderance of evidence, he will get the death penalty for Eternity.

- His defense will largely come from his Pastor and their place of worship. It is located at 666 Broadway Ave North. Upon research it is listed in the Statutes § Mt. 7:13-14. At that location it mentions the Broad Way avenue and it's activities.

- Humans have become very knowledgeable throughout history. However, that is if they are compared to other humans of less intelligence, or to the animals. The greatest advances made was in the area of computers. They created a tiny device called a Flash or Jump Drive that can download nearly the entire data from a computer. This device is smaller than one of the fingers that plugged it into the computer port to steal the information.

- Now comes the startling revelation that God designed a Flash much smaller, about the size of one cell. He installed it inside the brain of every human-being that ever lived. This Jump Drive or Flash is so powerful that it has recorded not only every word spoken by that individual, but also every thought and every motive and attitude behind every action.

- ***But I say unto you, That every idle word that men shall speak, they shall give account thereof in the day of judgment. For by thy words thou shalt be justified, and by thy words thou shalt be condemned.*** Statute § Matthew 12:36-37

- We will now begin this court hearing by pulling this Flash from Mr. Luke Wahrm and play it now in full color, starting from his birth.

HOLY SPIRIT: Now that we have viewed this video of Mr. Luke's life, we can easily see why he came to receive such a name. He never seriously dedicated his life to spiritual zeal.

DEFENSE, VEHR: On the contrary my client, Luke, has always come to me for council. When we held a large revival a few years ago, I asked if there was anyone that wanted to receive Christ into their life? Luke was the first to raise his hand.

HOLY SPIRIT: True, but this complex Flash drive exposed his motive for doing it. Instead of remorse and conviction for his sins, he had a smile on his face when he raised his hand. A smile is not what condemns or justifies a person, but the attitude behind it does. Anyone that saw that video can see the publicity motive that he was accomplishing for his action. He didn't accept Christ that day, but relished the praise of men. He wasn't cold against the things of God, but he also was never hot for God either. At best, he was always Luke-warm! Statute § Revelation 3:16

HOLY SPIRIT: Watching his life go by, as in a flash of time on this Flash drive, his desires and actions to steal from others became a way with him since a child. He stole from his boss and company. He stole whenever the opportunity was there, and when he desired the possession.

DEFENSE, D.C.VEHR: Sure my client had a problem with stealing. But, of the sins listed, I don't recall seeing "stealing" on that list of actions that would send my client to a fire & brimstone eternity.

HOLY SPIRIT: It is natural for people to want something. However, it is wrong to covet and envy something so strongly that they steal it from the owner. Remember what he told his buddy at the same work place? They agreed together that they need to work together to "replace" two large objects from their company. Their team-work allowed them to accomplish it. They "replaced" that merchandise from the company's place, to their place.

HOLY SPIRIT: Mr. Luke's worst characteristics are/is with his drunkenness and revellings. I am alarmed that often his Defense Council, Mr. Vehr, would be participating alongside of Luke in this drinking environment.

DEFENSE, VEHR: OBJECT! I am also his pastor and I know that Jesus made wine! Just because we enjoy a few beers together and get a little noisy, you can't possibly condemn us for that. After all, we are not drunk! We are not murderers!

HOLY SPIRIT: I will not get into what type of wine Jesus made. But I will ask both of you where in the Bible did Jesus make beer, Margaritas, Martinis, or whiskey? Isn't that what you consume usually? When you were living on Earth, Law Enforcement would declare Drunk Driving at the highest at .08% and much lower in many circumstances. So if man has declared it as drunkenness, do you still claim that you don't exceed that percentage at least on a monthly basis, if not every Friday night? If you do exceed, doesn't even man declare you as drunk?

HOLY SPIRIT: We could continue with the hatred which you have toward certain individuals. How about the affairs you have had. Pastor Vehr, you have declared your opinion onto Mr. Luke that when a person gets saved from their sins, it includes all the future sins until your natural death. Where do you find that verse in the Bible "Statutes"? Is it a lie? And if it is, Mr. Luke, are you a lover of that lie? So according to Statute § James 2:10 – *For whosoever shall keep the whole law, and yet offend in one point, he is guilty of all. SO, HONORABLE GOD, THIS IS MY CLOSING ARGUMENT.*

PRESIDING HONORABLE, GOD: I find the evidence against Mr. Luke Wahrm overwhelming toward his conviction. Even though he didn't commit murder, he is guilty of it which includes being a partaker of all twenty-four stones of Eternal death. Therefore, I sentence him to the Fire & Brimstone Prison for a complete Eternal Life sentence without parole. To complete this hearing for Mr. Luke, I will refer to the last two words following the Statute § Revelation 22:21,....

THE END

DISCLAIMER

According to 1 Corinthians 13:12, humans may not understand everything exactly like God sees things. ***For now we see through a glass, darkly; but then face to face: now I know in part; but then shall I know even as also I am known.*** Jesus told his disciples several things and yet they didn't comprehend things correctly. I, Bernie Tocholke, believe the things written in this book might be on the stricter side at the final judgment. However, I hope I am wrong and the opposite bookend of extreme tolerance is a more correct interpretation. Suppose you resisted and fought against all Cyanide Pie and made it to heaven. Would you be disappointed if you found out then that the requirement was extremely easy and Grace covered everything? On the other hand, what would you do if you Feasted on the Cherry Pie and at the judgment found out that the scriptures presented in this book are absolutely correct and extremely restrictive? You, the reader, must now decide where you will place the degree of judgment severity for that future event. You have to be right. Eternity is way too long to be wrong.